Easy French
Country Classics

THE KNAPP PRESS

PUBLISHERS

LOS ANGELES

Published by The Knapp Press
5900 Wilshire Boulevard, Los Angeles, California 90036

Library of Congress Cataloging in Publication Data

Main entry under title:
Easy French country classics.
(Quick cuisine international)
Includes index.
1. Cookery, French.   I. Series.
TX719.E27   1984   641.5944   84–14391
ISBN 0–89535–146–3

On the cover: *Romaine Soufflé*

Recipes developed by Helen Eldridge
Recipes on pages 13, 37, 57, 61, 73, 79, 81, and 113 developed by
Lorraine Shapiro
Cover photograph: Henry Bjoin
Food stylist: Birthe Foreman

Printed and bound in the United States of America

10   9   8   7   6   5   4   3   2   1

Contents

Introduction

I grew up in a family that revered good food—especially the honest, heartwarming cuisine of provincial France. My grandmother, who came to this country from Normandy as a young woman, is expert at slowly, carefully preparing the rich sauces and soufflés, the robust stews, and the hearty soups that are hallmarks of French country cooking. Under her guidance, my mother also became an accomplished cook, and she in turn brought me up with a deep love of our culinary heritage.

Although I long ago learned the techniques of French provincial cooking, the real essence of this cuisine is *time*, and, with a young son and a growing career, I've found that I have less and less time to spend in the kitchen. Not wanting to give up my favorite cuisine, I've collected the recipes I like best—many of them my mother's and my grandmother's— and selected those that were already quick or that could be speeded up by altering the method, without reducing the quality. The result is *Easy French Country Classics*, a compilation of the best and the quickest recipes I know for authentic French country cooking.

With *Easy French Country Classics* as inspiration, you'll be able to prepare delicious authentic French dishes in less time than you ever thought possible. You can impress your family and friends with homemade Turkey Breast Pâté (page 17), ready to serve in only fifteen minutes. In less than an hour, you can delight your guests with savory Chicken with Wine Vinegar Glaze (page 63) or a classic, irresistible Quiche Lorraine (page 79). Round out your menus with a wonderful side dish, such as vividly flavored Spiced Vegetables (page 95). And no one will be able to pass up dessert when presented with spectacular Pears Belle Hélène (page 113).

My goal in creating this book was to provide shortcuts to French country cuisine; instead of shortcuts, however, I think I've come up with what are actually *better* methods. It's old world tradition with modern convenience; the quality of authentic provincial cooking without the hours in the kitchen. *Easy French Country Classics* helps me face daily meal planning with confidence and impromptu entertaining without panic. It's my answer to the problem of no time. I hope it will be yours, too.

—*Michelle Garner*

" . . . a perfect appetizer, light, delicious, and quick."

Mushroom and Herb Rolls

4 servings

1 **tablespoon minced shallot *or* green onion, white part only**
1 **tablespoon butter**
¼ **pound mushrooms, finely chopped**
1 **teaspoon lemon juice**
1 **teaspoon mixed dried herbs, any combination of dill, basil, tarragon *or* oregano**
1 **package garlic and herb cream cheese (3.5 ounces)**
½ **package frozen puff pastry (17¼-ounce package)**
1 **egg mixed with 1 tablespoon water (egg wash)**

1 Preheat oven to 425°F. Sauté shallot or onion in butter until soft, about 5 minutes.

2 Add mushrooms and lemon juice and cook until mushrooms are soft and juices absorbed. Add herbs, mix well and set aside to cool.

3 Mix cream cheese with cooled mushrooms. Adjust seasonings to taste.

4 Roll out puff pastry to 10 × 12-inch rectangle. Spread with filling and cut into fifteen 2 × 4-inch rectangles.

5 Roll up each rectangle and brush with egg wash.

6 Place seam side down on ungreased baking sheet. Bake until golden, about 15 minutes. Serve immediately.

*" . . . my own version of the popular garlic
and herb cheese."*

Herbed Cheese
from Provence

Makes 1 cup

7 **ounces triple cream cheese,
room temperature**
1 **tablespoon finely minced
fresh parsley**
1 **teaspoon finely minced fresh
dill**
1 **large clove garlic, minced**
½ **teaspoon Herbes de Provence**
½ **teaspoon dried thyme**
⅛ **teaspoon pepper**

1 Place cream cheese in a bowl and with a fork blend in parsley, dill, garlic, Herbes de Provence, thyme and pepper.

2 Turn into a small crock or soufflé dish.

3 Serve at room temperature or chilled, with raw vegetables or crackers. If chilled several hours, let stand at room temperature for 15 minutes before serving.

*"These crisp puffs are much quicker than
my grandmother's traditional gougère ring."*

Gougères

Makes 24 to 30

1 tablespoon Dijon-style mustard
¼ teaspoon dry mustard
⅛ teaspoon salt
1½ tablespoons sugar
Dash of ground red pepper
¼ cup (½ stick) butter, cut into 8 pieces
½ cup water, chilled
½ cup all purpose unbleached flour
2 large eggs, room temperature
½ cup plus 2 tablespoons shredded Gruyère cheese
1 egg whisked with ½ eggshell of water (egg wash)

1 Preheat oven to 375°F. Combine mustards, salt, sugar and ground red pepper; set aside.

2 Lightly butter 2 baking sheets.

3 Place water and butter in 2-quart saucepan and bring to a boil.

4 Stir in flour quickly and beat over low heat until mixture is smooth and comes away from sides of pan, forming a ball.

5 Beat in mustard mixture and eggs, one at a time, beating well after each addition. After adding last egg, beat until mixture has satinlike sheen. Beat in ½ cup Gruyère.

6 Spoon into 24 to 30 little mounds, keeping each as high as possible. Paint with egg wash and sprinkle with remaining Gruyère.

7 Bake for 30 minutes. Remove puffs from oven and slit. Return to oven for 5 minutes. Immediately remove from pans. Serve warm or at room temperature.

*"Traditional pâtés take hours to prepare;
this is ready in minutes."*

Turkey Breast Pâté

6 to 8 servings
Freezes well for up to 1 month.

1½ **cups cooked turkey** *or* **chicken breast, cut into cubes**
  1 **tablespoon minced onion**
  ½ **cup (1 stick) butter**
  2 **teaspoons lemon juice**
  ¼ **teaspoon salt**
  ⅛ **teaspoon white pepper**
2½ **teaspoons anchovy paste**
  Chopped fresh parsley (garnish)

1 With motor running, drop turkey and onion into bowl of processor fitted with steel knife.

2 Remove top and add remaining ingredients except parsley. Process until very fine.

3 Adjust seasoning to taste. Chill 30 minutes. Garnish with parsley.

4 Serve on hot, thin toast, French bread, thin pumpernickel slices or whole wheat crackers.

"A great first course for an impromptu dinner."

Mushrooms Stuffed with Clams

6 servings
Serve as appetizers or with fish.

12 **large mushrooms (about 2½ inches), caps left whole, stems removed and finely chopped**
¼ **cup minced shallot**
3 **tablespoons butter**
1 **large garlic clove, minced**
1 **slice good white bread, coarsely crumbled *or* cut into tiny cubes**
1 **6½-ounce can of minced clams, drained**
2 **tablespoons finely chopped fresh parsley**
3 **tablespoons white wine, or to taste**
¾ **teaspoon finely chopped fresh tarragon *or* ¼ teaspoon dried**
1 **egg yolk**
3 **tablespoons whipping cream Salt and pepper to taste**
3 **tablespoons grated Parmesan cheese**

1 Sauté chopped mushroom stems with shallot in half the butter until shallot is tender, adding garlic halfway through.

2 Add bread, clams, 1 tablespoon parsley, wine and tarragon.

3 Beat egg yolk very well with cream. Remove clam mixture from heat and add egg yolk–cream mixture.

4 Return to heat and cook for 1 minute only.

5 Adjust seasoning to taste. Preheat oven to 350°F.

6 Melt remaining butter and brush mushroom caps with it. Turn caps hollow side up and fill with stuffing, mounding it. Sprinkle with Parmesan cheese.

7 Bake until heated through, 10 to 15 minutes. Sprinkle with remaining parsley.

" . . . also perfect for a light summer lunch."

Shrimp and Scallops Rémoulades

8 to 12 servings

¼ **cup Dijon-style mustard**
½ **cup olive oil**
¼ **cup white wine vinegar**
½ **teaspoon salt**
¼ **teaspoon pepper**
2 **teaspoons superfine sugar**
1 **tablespoon finely chopped fresh dill**
¼ **cup finely chopped shallot**
¼ **cup chopped fresh parsley, plus additional for garnish**
1 **pound cooked bay scallops**
1½ **pounds cooked shelled medium shrimp**
Dill *or* other fresh greens

1 Using processor or blender, mix together all ingredients except scallops and shrimp.

2 Adjust seasoning to taste.

3 Pour mixture over scallops and shrimp.

4 Chill for 2 to 3 hours, gently tossing from time to time to make sure seafood is well marinated.

5 Place in chilled bowl lined with dill or other greens.

6 Sprinkle with parsley and serve with cocktail picks.

"As a child, I would sneak these from my mother's appetizer tray when she was entertaining."

Roquefort Tarts

4 ounces Roquefort cheese, mashed
3 tablespoons butter, room temperature
1 ounce Cognac *or* Armagnac
White pepper to taste
2 ounces walnuts, lightly toasted and coarsely chopped (optional) (toast 6 to 8 minutes at 350°F)
12 thin slices French bread

1 Preheat oven to 350°F. Blend together Roquefort, butter and Cognac.

2 Add pepper and walnuts.

3 Toast slices of bread. While still hot, spread with Roquefort mixture. (Or pretoast the bread lightly, spread with Roquefort mixture and heat in oven 1 to 2 minutes.)

" . . . a heady garlic mayonnaise that was a staple in my grandmother's kitchen."

Aïoli

Makes 1¾ cups
(enough for 12 servings)

4 **large garlic cloves**
¾ **teaspoon salt**
3 **egg yolks, room temperature**
1½ **cups olive oil *or***
combination of olive and
peanut oils
1½ **tablespoons lemon juice**
⅛ **teaspoon white pepper**

1 Peel garlic cloves and mince in processor or crush in press.

2 Add salt and pulverize in a mortar and pestle until garlic becomes a puree.

3 With motor running, place egg yolks in processor.

4 After a few seconds, add garlic paste.

5 In a very fine stream, very slowly and gradually add half the oil.

6 Gradually add lemon juice and then remaining oil. Season with pepper.

7 Serve with raw vegetables, on fish, on boiled potatoes, as sandwich spread, or spread on croutons for soup.

*"This spicy sauce from Provence adds a
little spark to soups."*

Rouille

Makes 1 cup (enough for 8 servings)
All ingredients must be at room temperature.

 4 **garlic cloves**
 ½ **teaspoon salt**
 2 **egg yolks, room temperature**
    Lemon juice
 ½ **teaspoon ground red pepper**
 ¼ **teaspoon saffron threads** *or*
    dash powdered saffron
 1 **cup olive oil**
 2 **tablespoons coarsely chopped**
    red bell pepper *or* **pimiento**
    (seed before chopping)

1 Peel garlic cloves and mince in processor or crush in press.

2 Sprinkle garlic with salt and mash in a mortar and pestle until garlic becomes a puree.

3 Place egg yolks, 1 tablespoon lemon juice, garlic paste, ground red pepper and saffron in bowl of processor. Process and scrape bowl. Repeat.

4 With motor running, very slowly pour in the olive oil.

5 Process until mixture has homogenized and thickened. Adjust sauce to taste with lemon juice and/ or salt. Mix in red bell pepper or pimiento. Stir into soups to taste, or serve on fish.

"I adapted this from my aunt Cécille's recipe. She would make large batches and freeze it."

Cream of Asparagus Soup

6 servings

3 tablespoons unsalted butter 2 cups minced onion 4 cups chicken stock 1¼ pounds fresh thin asparagus, trimmed ¼ cup Crème Fraîche (see recipe, page 105) *or* whipping cream ¾ teaspoon salt ¼ teaspoon white pepper Lemon juice (optional)	**1** Melt butter in 4-quart pan. Add onion and cook slowly just until soft and golden; do not brown. **2** Add chicken stock and bring to a boil. **3** Meanwhile, cut tips (about 3 inches in length) off asparagus and set aside. In processor or blender or by hand, slice butt ends into ¼-inch pieces. **4** Drop pieces into boiling broth. Cover and boil gently until very soft, about 30 minutes. **5** Cool for 10 minutes, then puree soup in blender or processor. **6** Return soup to pan. Add asparagus tips and simmer until just tender, about 5 minutes. **7** Stir in cream. Season with salt and pepper and a drop or two of lemon juice. Serve warm or cold.

" . . . a piquant and creamy cold soup."

Red Bell Pepper Soup

6 to 8 servings
Prepare at least 3 hours in advance.

⅓ cup (⅔ stick) butter
4 cups chopped red bell pepper (seed before chopping)
2 cups sliced leeks (white and pale green parts only)
1½ cups chicken stock
4 cups buttermilk
Salt and white pepper to taste
Hot pepper sauce to taste
1 bunch chives, finely chopped (garnish)

1 Melt butter in a nonaluminum 2½- to 3-quart saucepan.

2 Add chopped peppers and leeks and sauté over medium heat until soft but not brown.

3 Add chicken stock and bring to boil. Reduce heat and simmer for 30 minutes with lid of pan ajar.

4 Cool 15 minutes. Puree in processor in batches until mixture is very smooth.

5 When mixture is at room temperature, stir in buttermilk and add salt and pepper and hot pepper sauce. Strain.

6 Chill for at least 3 hours or for as long as 24 hours. Garnish with a sprinkle of chives.

" . . . a homely vegetable that makes a beautiful soup."

Celery Root Soup

8 servings

1	**large (½ pound) russet potato, peeled and cubed**
1½	**to 2 pounds (3 medium) celery root (celeriac), peeled and cubed**
1	**tablespoon butter**
1	**cup finely sliced leek (white and light green parts only)**
4	**cups unsalted chicken stock**
¼	**cup whipping cream**
	Salt and white pepper to taste
1½	**tablespoons chopped fresh chives (garnish)**

1 As you prepare them, drop potato and celery root into bowl of cold water. Set aside.

2 Melt butter in medium stockpot; add leek and cook, without browning, about 5 minutes.

3 Add chicken stock, potato and celery root. Cover and bring to a boil.

4 Reduce heat to a simmer and cook about 25 minutes. Remove from heat and let cool about 5 minutes.

5 Puree in processor or blender.

6 Return soup to stockpot and add cream and salt and pepper. (If soup is too thick, thin with chicken stock.) Heat gently to serving temperature. Pour into soup bowls and garnish each serving with chopped chives.

"This soup will surprise you. It's absolutely delicious!"

Cream of Radish Leaf Soup

8 to 10 servings

2 tablespoons butter
1 large onion, chopped
2 bunches radish leaves, chopped
2 garlic cloves, minced
4 tomatoes, peeled and chopped
1½ quarts vegetable water *or* beef *or* chicken stock
¼ cup uncooked rice
1 large russet potato, peeled and chopped
½ cup whipping cream *or* Crème Fraîche (see recipe, page 105)
Salt and white pepper to taste
Sliced radishes (garnish)
Chopped fresh parsley (garnish)

1 Melt butter in heavy saucepan. Add onion and cook until tender but not brown.

2 Add radish leaves; cook until wilted.

3 Add garlic and tomatoes; cook 3 minutes.

4 Add stock, rice and potato; bring to boil, reduce heat and simmer about 40 minutes.

5 Put through blender or processor in batches.

6 When soup is smooth, return to pan and heat almost to boiling, stirring constantly. Remove from heat.

7 Stir in cream and adjust seasoning to taste.

8 Pour into soup bowls and garnish each serving with radishes and parsley.

"Watercress adds a distinctive touch to this classic soup."

Watercress Vichyssoise

6 **cups chicken stock**
2 **medium boiling potatoes**
4 **cups coarsely chopped leek**
2 **cups lightly packed watercress sprigs**
½ **cup whipping cream**
1¼ **teaspoons salt**
½ **teaspoon white pepper**
Watercress sprigs (garnish)

1 Bring chicken stock to a boil. Add potatoes and leek, return to boil, then reduce heat. Cover and simmer 20 minutes or until potatoes are tender.

2 Briefly immerse watercress sprigs in boiling water. Drain and immediately immerse in ice water. Drain and add to soup.

3 In a food processor or blender, puree soup in batches. Turn into a bowl. Stir in cream and salt and pepper. Chill.

4 Serve in chilled soup bowls and garnish with watercress sprigs.

"I use a processor to speed up this family recipe."

Provençale Vinaigrette

Makes 1 pint

2 eggs
1½ cups olive *or* vegetable oil
1 teaspoon salt
½ teaspoon white pepper
2 garlic cloves, finely minced
2 tablespoons lemon juice
¼ cup wine vinegar
2 teaspoons anchovy paste *or* half of 2-ounce can anchovy fillets

1 Using a blender or processor, whip eggs until light and frothy.

2 *Gradually* add oil in a thin stream and process until mixture thickens.

3 Gradually add remaining ingredients and adjust seasoning. (May need thinning with ½ tablespoon water.)

4 Chill at least 45 minutes.

5 Serve over mixed greens, such as green leaf, butter, salad bowl and romaine lettuce, watercress and spinach, plus artichoke hearts, thinly sliced scallions, or other vegetables.

*"I've served this salad at every meal
except breakfast."*

Vermicelli Salad
à la Baumanière

8 servings

1 **large chicken breast**
2 **6½-ounce jars marinated artichoke hearts, coarsely chopped**
¾ **cup tightly packed fresh basil leaves, shredded**
1½ **cups Provençale Vinaigrette (see recipe, page 39)**
8 **ounces vermicelli (uncooked)**
1 **tablespoon, plus ½ teaspoon salt**
1 **tablespoon olive *or* vegetable oil**
½ **cup chopped fresh parsley, plus additional for garnish**
4 **tomatoes, peeled, juiced, seeded and cut into small strips**
⅛ **teaspoon white pepper Lemon juice (optional)**

1 Poach chicken breast until just cooked, 15 to 20 minutes. Shred coarsely.

2 Combine chicken and artichoke hearts in a large bowl along with a little of the artichoke marinade.

3 Add ½ cup basil and a little Provençale Vinaigrette and mix well.

4 Break vermicelli in half or in thirds and add to 5 to 6 quarts boiling water along with 1 tablespoon salt and oil. Cook to al dente stage, 4 to 5 minutes.

5 Drain, rinse briefly in cold water and drain again.

6 Quickly mix with chicken, adding more vinaigrette as needed.

7 Just before serving, add parsley, remaining ¼ cup basil and tomatoes. Toss. Garnish with remaining parsley.

8 Adjust seasoning to taste with salt and white pepper and lemon juice.

*"An unlikely combination, but well worth
the risk!"*

Orange and Onion Salad

6 servings

1 small head curly endive (chicory), inside leaves only	**1** Arrange bed of torn chicory on platter.
3 seedless oranges, peeled and sliced ¼ inch thick	**2** Top with overlapping orange slices and garnish with onion.
½ small red onion, finely sliced	**3** Blend remaining ingredients well and drizzle over onion and orange slices.
½ teaspoon dry mustard	
½ teaspoon paprika	**4** Chill about 30 minutes, tossing gently from time to time.

1 small head curly endive
(chicory), inside leaves only
3 seedless oranges, peeled and
sliced ¼ inch thick
½ small red onion, finely sliced
½ teaspoon dry mustard
½ teaspoon paprika
½ teaspoon salt
¼ cup red wine vinegar
½ cup olive oil

1 Arrange bed of torn chicory on platter.

2 Top with overlapping orange slices and garnish with onion.

3 Blend remaining ingredients well and drizzle over onion and orange slices.

4 Chill about 30 minutes, tossing gently from time to time.

"*This Spanish-style salad comes from the
south of France.*"

Andalusian Salad

⅓ cup thinly sliced radish

1 cup finely sliced celery

2 tablespoons finely chopped fresh parsley, plus additional for garnish

⅓ cup chopped scallion

2 cups steamed brown *or* white rice

½ cup raisins

½ cup sunflower seeds

½ teaspoon salt

¼ teaspoon coarsely ground pepper

½ teaspoon sugar

1½ tablespoons red wine vinegar

6 tablespoons olive oil

¼ pound mushrooms, finely sliced

1 head butter lettuce

1 In bowl, combine radish, celery, parsley, scallion, rice, raisins and sunflower seeds. Set aside.

2 In separate bowl or in jar with tight-fitting lid, mix salt and pepper, sugar and vinegar; blend until salt and sugar are dissolved. Add oil and stir or shake well.

3 Pour enough dressing over vegetable mixture to moisten. Chill for at least 30 minutes.

4 Just before serving, add mushrooms and toss.

5 Arrange on lettuce leaves on individual plates or in a bowl. Garnish with parsley.

" . . . the French ancestor of the familiar three-bean salad."

Belle Vue Salad

8 servings

1 8-ounce can garbanzo beans (chick-peas)
1 16-ounce can red kidney beans
1 scallion, thinly sliced
Garlic Dressing (see following recipe)
½ to 1 pound fresh green beans (preferably Kentucky Wonder *or* tiny French)
1 red bell pepper, cut into ⅛-inch strips
½ head (or more) curly endive (chicory), torn into small pieces

Garlic Dressing
Makes about 1 cup
¼ cup red wine vinegar
1 teaspoon sugar
2 medium cloves garlic, chopped
¼ teaspoon pepper
½ teaspoon salt, or to taste
1 egg yolk
¾ cup olive oil

1 Drain garbanzo and kidney beans. Rinse and drain again.

2 Add scallion and enough Garlic Dressing to coat well. Marinate for at least 15 minutes.

3 Cook green beans until crisp-tender and then let cool. Cut into 2-inch lengths and toss with bean-scallion mixture.

4 Add pepper strips and endive and more dressing if desired.

5 Toss. Adjust seasoning to taste.

1 Place all ingredients except oil in blender or processor and process briefly.

2 With motor running, *slowly* pour in oil and process about 30 seconds.

3 Adjust seasoning to taste.

*"In the Continental fashion, I serve this
after dinner with cheese."*

Grapefruit, Apple and Grape Salad

May be served after the main course.
6 servings

2 **tart red apples**
Dressing (see following recipe)
½ **pound blue grapes, halved and seeded, *or* seedless red grapes, halved**
1 **grapefruit, peeled and sectioned, membrane removed**
1 **bunch watercress**

Dressing
2 **tablespoons lemon juice**
2 **teaspoons superfine sugar**
2 **tablespoons fruit brandy (such as Grand Marnier *or* kirsh)**

1 Core apples and cut into eighths. Immediately coat with Dressing.

2 Combine fruits and add just enough Dressing to coat. Chill for at least 15 minutes.

3 Arrange with watercress on individual plates or in a shallow bowl.

1 Put ingredients in jar with tight-fitting lid and shake well.

"This hearty salad, accompanied with crusty French bread and dry white wine, is a meal in itself."

Country Chef's Salad

6 servings

1 **small head romaine lettuce, torn into medium pieces**
1 **small head red-leaf lettuce, torn into medium pieces**
1 **bunch watercress**
¼ **cup fresh tarragon leaves**
1 **cup thinly sliced mushrooms**
¼ **pound Swiss cheese, cut into ½-inch dice**
¼ **pound French sausage *or* Genoa salami, sliced into thin strips**
½ **to 1 pound cooked chicken breast *or* turkey breast, cubed**
2 **hard-cooked eggs, quartered (garnish)**
1 **or 2 avocados, sliced (garnish)**

Dressing
Makes about 1 cup
¼ **cup red wine vinegar *or* raspberry vinegar**
¾ **cup olive oil**
½ **teaspoon salt**
1 **tablespoon Dijon-style mustard**
1 **teaspoon sugar**
¼ **teaspoon pepper**

1 In large, shallow bowl, mix greens and tarragon.

2 Arrange mushrooms, cheese, sausage and chicken or turkey on top of greens.

3 Garnish with slices of egg and avocado and sprinkle lightly with Dressing.

4 Toss salad just before serving and add more Dressing if needed.

1 Combine ingredients in jar with tight-fitting lid and shake vigorously.

"Spinach salads abound, but this one is, I think, exceptionally good."

Spinach Salad

1½ cups sliced Jerusalem
   artichoke (also called
   sunchoke)
2 tablespoons lemon juice
1 bunch (¾ pound) fresh
   spinach, washed and dried
4 strips bacon, chopped and
   cooked until crisp
¼ pound mushrooms, thinly
   sliced
1 large scallion, thinly sliced

Dressing
Makes ¾ cup
2 tablespoons red wine
   vinegar
1 tablespoon Dijon-style
   mustard
1 teaspoon sugar
1 small egg yolk
⅓ cup olive oil
   Salt and pepper to taste

1 Marinate Jerusalem artichoke in lemon juice for 10 minutes.

2 Toss lightly with spinach, bacon, mushrooms and scallion.

3 Coat lightly with Dressing.

1 Whisk together vinegar, mustard, sugar and egg yolk.

2 Gradually whisk in olive oil. Season to taste.

Endive, Tomato and Watercress Salad

4 to 6 servings

1 tablespoon lemon juice
1 teaspoon Dijon-style mustard
   Salt and pepper to taste
¼ cup light olive oil
3 small Belgian endive, leaves separated
1 to 1½ bunches watercress, heavy stems removed
4 medium tomatoes, peeled, seeded and coarsely chopped
   Minced fresh parsley (garnish)

1 Blend lemon juice, mustard and salt and pepper and whisk in oil.

2 When ready to serve, place endive on a plate, arranged like spokes of a wheel; then place watercress in center and top with tomatoes.

3 Sprinkle dressing over salad and garnish with parsley.

*"A classic salad that offers great creative
possibilities in the presentation."*

Salade Niçoise

4 to 6 servings

1 **pound small potatoes, cooked until tender**
1 **tablespoon minced scallion**
¼ **teaspoon salt**
⅛ **teaspoon pepper**
¼ **cup dry white wine Dressing (see following recipe)**
½ **pound fresh green beans, blanched, chilled and cut into 2-inch pieces**
1 **head Boston lettuce, chilled**
2 **or 3 medium tomatoes, cut into wedges**
2 **or 3 hard-cooked eggs, quartered**
1 **2-ounce can anchovy fillets**
2 **tablespoons capers**
1 **7-ounce can water-packed albacore (tuna), drained**
½ **cup Niçoise or ripe olives**
2 **to 3 tablespoons minced fresh parsley**

Dressing
Makes ⅔ cup
½ **cup olive oil**
1 **tablespoon white wine vinegar**
1 **tablespoon lemon juice**
¼ **teaspoon salt**
⅛ **teaspoon pepper**
¼ **teaspoon dry mustard**

1 Peel potatoes and cut in half lengthwise, then slice ⅜ inch thick.

2 Place in a large bowl. Add green onion, salt and pepper and wine. Toss gently. Let stand 5 minutes, tossing again, until liquid is absorbed.

3 Pour ¼ cup Dressing over potatoes and toss gently to blend. Taste and adjust seasoning. Cover and refrigerate.

4 Marinate green beans in a little of Dressing in refrigerator.

5 Arrange lettuce in large salad bowl or deep platter. Place potatoes in center. Arrange green beans and tomatoes around potatoes. Place eggs, yolk side up, at intervals. Top with anchovies and capers. Place chunks of tuna around edge or in center of potatoes. Ring potatoes with olives. Sprinkle with Dressing and parsley.

1 Combine oil, vinegar, lemon juice, salt and pepper and mustard in a small bowl and blend with whisk.

*"The delicate tarragon butter discs melting
on the fillets are a mouth-watering sight."*

Fish Fillets with Tarragon Butter

4 to 5 servings

2 tablespoons white wine vinegar *or* tarragon vinegar
½ teaspoon dried tarragon *or* 1 teaspoon fresh, chopped
½ cup (1 stick) butter, cut into 8 pieces
1½ pounds fish fillets, such as red snapper, scrod, sea bass *or* sea trout
2 tablespoons vegetable oil
Salt and white pepper to taste
Paprika
2 to 3 tablespoons chopped fresh parsley

1 Put vinegar and tarragon in a small pan and boil until reduced by about two-thirds. Over very low heat whisk in butter, one piece at a time, letting each piece dissolve before adding next piece.

2 Chill mixture in a small bowl until firm enough to roll into a cylinder about 1 inch thick, about 30 minutes. Wrap cylinder in plastic wrap and chill at least 15 minutes. With a sharp knife dipped in hot water, slice cylinder into thin discs about ⅛ inch thick. Refrigerate until ready to serve fish.

3 Preheat broiler. Brush fish with oil, season lightly with salt and pepper and paprika and place on oiled broiler pan. Cook about 4 inches from heat for 6 to 8 minutes, watching carefully. (Fish may be baked instead in preheated 450°F oven 8 to 10 minutes.)

4 Top fillets with tarragon butter discs, sprinkle lightly with paprika and serve immediately.

"...quick, cool, and elegant. My mother's
Sauce Verte is the perfect accompaniment."

Poached Salmon with Sauce Verte

6 to 8 servings

2 cups water
1 cup dry white wine
1 small carrot, thinly sliced
1 small onion, thinly sliced
1 small stalk celery, thinly sliced
½ lemon, thinly sliced
3 sprigs parsley
1 bay leaf
8 peppercorns
½ teaspoon salt
¼ teaspoon thyme
1 2-pound salmon
   Lemon wedges (garnish)
   Watercress *or* fresh dill (garnish)

1 Combine water, wine, carrot, onion, celery, lemon, parsley, bay leaf, peppercorns, salt and thyme in poacher. Cover and simmer 15 minutes.

2 Measure depth of fish at thickest part. Place fish on poacher rack and set into simmering liquid. When simmering resumes, poach 10 minutes per inch, about 20 to 25 minutes for a 2-pound salmon. Salmon is done when fish flakes when prodded with fork in thickest section and flesh turns pale pink near bone.

3 Lift salmon on rack and slip onto serving platter. Peel and discard exposed skin. Garnish with lemon wedges and watercress or dill. Serve warm or cold with Sauce Verte.

Sauce Verte

Makes ¾ cup

1½ cups watercress leaves
1½ tablespoons finely minced fresh parsley
1½ tablespoons finely minced fresh dill
1 teaspoon minced fresh basil
½ cup mayonnaise
1 tablespoon lemon juice
1 tablespoon Dijon-style mustard

1 Immerse watercress briefly in boiling water, then plunge into ice water. Remove and squeeze dry. Place in food processor or blender with parsley, dill and basil. Process until finely minced.

2 Combine with mayonnaise in a bowl. Blend in lemon juice and mustard.

" . . . a wonderfully savory dish that originated—
according to my grandmother—
in the Armagnac region of France."

Chicken with
Red Wine Vinegar Glaze

4 to 6 servings

2 tablespoons butter
3 pounds chicken breasts and
  thighs, boned and skinned
  Salt and pepper to taste
6 garlic cloves, minced
⅓ cup raspberry *or* red wine
  vinegar
3 tablespoons Armagnac *or*
  Cognac
1 teaspoon tomato paste
2 teaspoons Dijon-style
  mustard
⅔ cup Crème Fraîche (see
  recipe, page 105) *or*
  whipping cream
2 medium tomatoes, peeled,
  juiced, seeded and diced
  Chopped fresh chervil *or*
  parsley (garnish)
  Sprigs of watercress
  (garnish)

1 Heat butter in a large sauté pan over moderate heat. Add chicken and sauté until brown, 4 or 5 minutes on each side. Season with salt and pepper.

2 Add garlic, cover pan and cook for about 20 minutes over low heat.

3 Remove chicken from pan and keep warm. Pour in vinegar and raise heat to high.

4 Stir vigorously, scraping pan to loosen caramelized juices on bottom and sides of pan. Reduce vinegar by three-quarters. Combine Armagnac, tomato paste and mustard and pour into sauté pan. Cook for several minutes, stirring constantly, then stir in cream. Pour glaze over chicken and sprinkle with tomato dice and a little chervil or parsley. Surround with watercress. Serve immediately.

*"...a real country dish, robust and
earthy. My husband loves it."*

Chicken with Garlic and Herbs

4 servings

4 garlic heads, boiled for 20 minutes
1 teaspoon salt
¼ teaspoon pepper
1 teaspoon dried rosemary *or* 3 teaspoons fresh
½ teaspoon dried marjoram *or* 1½ teaspoons fresh
1 teaspoon dried thyme *or* 3 teaspoons fresh
2 bay leaves, halved
⅓ cup olive oil
8 tiny artichokes, trimmed and halved
2½ pounds chicken parts
Watercress (garnish)

1 Preheat oven to 450°F. Cool garlic and remove husks, but not skin, from each clove.

2 Mix salt and pepper, garlic cloves and herbs with olive oil.

3 Pour a little of the oil mixture into a flameproof casserole. Add artichokes and chicken and pour remaining oil on top.

4 Stir thoroughly so that chicken and artichokes are well coated with oil, garlic and herbs.

5 Cover and place over high heat on top of stove. When oil begins to sizzle, place casserole in oven. Reduce heat to 375°F and bake for 45 minutes.

6 Before serving, remove bay leaves. Include garlic cloves, artichokes, and sauce with each portion; surround with watercress.

"This looks and tastes like a complicated gourmet recipe. It's actually quick and very easy."

Chicken in Port and Walnut Sauce

6 servings

3 large chicken breasts, boned, skinned and halved
All purpose flour
2 tablespoons butter
1 cup Port
2 cups chicken stock, boiled to reduce to 1 cup
1 cup Crème Fraîche (see recipe, page 105)
¼ teaspoon cracked pepper
½ cup walnuts, toasted and chopped (toast 10 minutes at 350°F)
4 strips bacon, cooked until crisp and chopped
Chopped fresh parsley (garnish)

1 Coat breasts lightly with flour. Sauté in butter until browned and cooked through, about 8 minutes. Remove from pan; keep warm.

2 Add Port and reduced chicken stock to pan and boil until reduced by half.

3 Whisk Crème Fraîche into stock and wine mixture and boil rapidly until mixture reaches a sauce consistency, about 10 minutes.

4 Stir in pepper, walnuts and bacon.

5 Pour a little sauce on each warmed dinner plate; place breast on top and cover with sauce. Garnish with parsley and serve immediately.

*" . . . another of my grandmother's recipes
which I've adapted."*

Basque-style Chicken

4 to 6 servings

1 cup dry white wine
2 tablespoons butter, melted
1 4-pound broiling chicken, cut into pieces
  Salt and pepper to taste
1 large onion, coarsely chopped
¼ cup olive oil
3 medium tomatoes, peeled, juiced and cut into eighths
¾ cup Spanish olives (mixture of black and green), pitted and sliced
⅔ cup slivered almonds, slightly toasted (toast 6 to 8 minutes at 350°F)
  Fresh parsley *or* watercress (garnish)

1 Preheat oven to 375°. Blend ½ cup wine with melted butter.

2 Season chicken with salt and pepper and place, skin down, in a lightly oiled shallow baking dish. Cover with butter-wine sauce.

3 Bake 25 minutes, basting once. Turn chicken, baste again, and cook until tender, about 15 minutes. After removing chicken, raise temperature to 400°F.

4 Meanwhile, in large skillet cook onion in olive oil until golden and tender. Stir in tomatoes, olives and remaining wine.

5 When chicken is tender, drain accumulated juices into pan with onion and olives. Cook sauce over high heat until slightly reduced and thickened. Adjust seasoning to taste.

6 Pour sauce over chicken and bake for 10 minutes.

7 Sprinkle with almonds and garnish with parsley or watercress.

*"This reminds me of large family
dinners at Easter. Everyone would
bring their special dish."*

Boned Lamb
Provençal Style

8 to 12 servings
Marinate several hours in advance or overnight.

1 5-pound leg of spring lamb,
  shaved of fell, defatted and
  boned
4 large garlic cloves, minced
1 2-ounce can anchovy fillets,
  plus half the oil
1 teaspoon fresh rosemary,
  chopped
3 tablespoons lemon juice
½ teaspoon pepper
¼ cup olive oil

1 Slash the two large lobes of meat in several places (otherwise, these thicker pieces will take longer to cook than the rest of the leg).

2 Mash garlic with anchovies and oil from anchovies into a smooth paste. Gradually work in rosemary, lemon juice and pepper. Add olive oil.

3 Rub marinade into all surfaces of prepared lamb leg. Let marinate, basting and turning occasionally.

4 Preheat oven to 375°F. Place lamb, boned side up, in shallow roasting pan. Pour marinade over and place in upper half of oven.

5 Roast to thermometer reading of 135–140°F, about 35 minutes, basting once or twice.

6 When lamb is done to taste, baste again and remove to a warm platter. Let stand for 10 minutes before slicing. Serve marinade juices separately as sauce.

*"The sauce turns this pepper steak into
a truly memorable dish."*

Pepper Steak

6 servings

1 tablespoon black peppercorns *or* 1 teaspoon *each* black, white and green peppercorns, coarsely crushed
2 1½-pound top sirloin steaks, New York *or* Spencer, trimmed and fat edges cut
2 tablespoons butter
1 tablespoon vegetable oil
2 tablespoons minced shallot or green onion (white part only)
¼ cup brandy
½ cup beef stock
2 tablespoons whipping cream or Crème Fraîche (see recipe, page 105)
Watercress (garnish)

1 Spread peppercorns out on large plate and turn meat in peppers. Press peppercorns firmly into meat with fingers and heel of hand. Let stand from 30 minutes to several hours in refrigerator.

2 Heat butter and oil in one or two large skillets over moderately high heat.

3 Add meat and sauté 3 to 5 minutes on each side for a 1-inch steak, 6 to 7 minutes for a 1½-inch steak. Remove to a hot platter and keep warm.

4 Sauté shallot in pan drippings until tender. Add brandy and set aflame, shaking pan.

5 Add beef stock and cook, stirring to loosen browned bits in bottom of pan. Boil until slightly reduced. Stir in cream.

6 Spoon sauce over meat. Garnish with watercress.

*"The French use tarragon in so many
recipes. This is one of my favorites."*

Veal in Tarragon Mushroom Sauce

4 servings

¾ to 1 pound veal scaloppine, cut into 1-inch slices and flattened to ¼-inch thickness
All purpose flour
Salt and pepper to taste
½ pound mushrooms, sliced
5 to 6 tablespoons clarified butter
1 teaspoon lemon juice
¼ cup finely chopped shallot
1 cup dry white wine
1 tablespoon chopped fresh tarragon *or* ½ teaspoon dried
1 cup beef stock
2 tablespoons Cognac
Dash of sugar
Glace de viande (optional)
Lemon juice
Watercress (garnish)

1 Dust veal with flour, season well with salt and pepper and set aside.

2 Brown mushrooms in 2 tablespoons clarified butter with lemon juice. Season lightly and set aside.

3 Cook shallot in 2 tablespoons clarified butter until soft but not brown. Add wine and tarragon; reduce to about 2 tablespoons.

4 Stir in beef stock and cook rapidly until slightly thickened, about 5 minutes.

5 Add mushrooms, Cognac and sugar to sauce. Add glace de viande, lemon juice and salt and pepper to taste.

6 Brown veal in clarified butter, cooking just until tender, about 5 minutes. Season lightly. Remove from pan and keep warm.

7 Pour some sauce on hot plates and arrange veal slices on them, placing a teaspoon of sauce on top of each, if desired. Garnish with watercress.

" . . . an old family favorite."

Roquefort-stuffed Pork Chops

4 servings

1 generous tablespoon minced onion
½ cup thinly sliced mushrooms
3 tablespoons butter
1 cup tiny bread cubes
½ cup crumbled Roquefort cheese
4 pork chops, 1 inch thick, cut with pockets for stuffing
Salt and white pepper to taste
Paprika
Watercress (garnish)

1 Sauté onion and mushrooms in butter for about 5 minutes; do not brown. Remove from heat and cool to lukewarm.

2 Preheat oven to 350°F. Add bread cubes and cheese to onion-mushroom mixture, stirring until blended.

3 Stuff chops and fasten with wood picks and string; season both sides with salt and pepper and paprika.

4 Bake, uncovered, in ovenproof dish for about 45 minutes.

5 Remove picks and string. Garnish with watercress and serve immediately.

"My grandmother, my mother, and my aunts all use this recipe. The filling is magnifique!*"*

Quiche Lorraine

4 to 6 servings

---

1 9-inch pie shell, partially
baked
1 egg white, slightly beaten
4 slices bacon
½ cup minced onion
1 cup shredded Swiss cheese
3 eggs
1 cup whipping cream
½ cup milk
¾ teaspoon salt
Dash of white pepper
Dash of nutmeg

1 Preheat oven to 375°F. Brush bottom of cooled pie shell with slightly beaten egg white to waterproof. Cook bacon until crisp. Remove from pan and reserve. Pour off drippings, saving 1 tablespoon.

2 Sauté onion in tablespoon of bacon drippings until tender. Arrange onion and bacon on bottom of pie shell and sprinkle with cheese.

3 Beat eggs with cream, milk, salt and pepper and nutmeg. Pour into pie shell.

4 Bake in upper third of oven until puffed and browned, 30 to 40 minutes. Knife inserted 1 inch from center should come out clean. Serve hot or cold.

*"I've had great ratatouille in the south
of France. This is my version."*

Ratatouille

2 medium eggplants (½ pound each), peeled
2 medium zucchini (½ pound each)
½ cup olive oil, or more
2 cloves garlic, minced
1 large onion, sliced
1 green bell pepper, sliced
4 medium tomatoes, peeled, seeded and sliced
1 teaspoon salt
¼ teaspoon pepper
1 small bay leaf, crumbled
½ teaspoon dried oregano
3 tablespoons minced fresh parsley

1 Preheat oven to 350°F. Cut eggplants and zucchini lengthwise into slices ⅜ inches thick, 3 inches long and 1 inch wide.

2 In hot olive oil slowly sauté eggplants until lightly browned, about 3 minutes on each side, adding more oil as needed. Remove and set aside. Sauté zucchini until lightly browned on each side, about 1 minute. Set aside.

3 In same skillet, sauté garlic, onion and green pepper until tender but not brown, about 10 minutes.

4 Add tomatoes and season with salt, pepper, bay leaf and oregano. Cover and cook over low heat until tomatoes render their juices, about 5 minutes.

5 Place one-third of tomatoes in bottom of a 7 × 11-inch baking dish and sprinkle with 1 tablespoon parsley. Arrange half of eggplants and zucchini on top. Repeat layers, ending with tomatoes and parsley.

6 Bake, basting occasionally, until most of juices have evaporated, about 30 minutes. Serve hot or cold.

" . . . a good basic rice dish."

Rice with Peas and Basil

3 **cups freshly steamed rice**
2 **tablespoons butter, room temperature**
2 **scallions, sliced**
1 **10½-ounce package frozen baby peas, thawed**
¼ **cup chopped fresh basil**
 Salt and white pepper to taste

1 Cook rice according to directions on package, then stir in butter until absorbed.

2 Add scallions, peas, basil and salt and pepper.

*" . . . a delicious accompaniment to almost
any main course."*

Tomatoes Provençal

3 firm ripe tomatoes, seeded, juiced and cut in half crosswise
Salt and pepper to taste
⅛ teaspoon sugar
½ cup dry breadcrumbs
¼ cup Pistou (see following recipe)
2 tablespoons olive oil
¼ cup pine nuts, toasted (toast 6 minutes at 350°F) (garnish)

1 Sprinkle tomatoes lightly with salt and pepper and sugar.

2 Mix breadcrumbs with Pistou and spread on tomatoes. Drizzle olive oil over tops.

3 Bake until tender, about 20 minutes. Garnish with pine nuts.

Pistou (Basil Sauce)
Makes about 1½ cups
1½ cups fresh basil leaves, loosely packed
½ cup coarsely chopped fresh parsley
¼ cup pine nuts
½ cup olive oil
3 garlic cloves, minced
⅔ cup combination of grated Parmesan and Romano cheese
2 tablespoons butter, room temperature

1 Place all ingredients except cheese and butter in processor, blender or mortar and pestle and process until smooth.

2 Add cheese and butter and process until thoroughly blended.

*"This is always a great success.
It's so delicious and unusual."*

Romaine Soufflé

6 to 8 servings

1 **head romaine lettuce (about ¾ pound), trimmed of stems and coarsely chopped**
4 **tablespoons (½ stick) butter**
¼ **cup chopped shallot *or* scallion**
3 **tablespoons all purpose flour**
1 **cup milk, heated**
1 **cup shredded cheddar *or* Gruyère cheese**
4 **egg yolks**
1 **teaspoon salt**
1 **teaspoon Worcestershire sauce**
8 **drops hot pepper sauce**
5 **egg whites**
  Grated Parmesan cheese (for pan and garnish)

1 Preheat oven to 400°F. Cook romaine in heavy saucepan until wilted. Drain well and chop fine.

2 Melt 1 tablespoon butter, add shallot and cook until soft. Add romaine and cook, stirring, until dry. Press out excess moisture in sieve.

3 In a separate saucepan, melt 3 tablespoons butter. Stir in flour and cook several minutes. Remove from heat and whisk in milk; return to heat and cook until thick. Add cheese.

4 Remove from heat and whisk in egg yolks one at a time; return to heat and cook 1 minute. Add romaine, salt, Worcestershire and pepper sauce. Adjust seasoning to taste.

5 Beat egg whites until stiff. Stir one-third into sauce, then fold the rest in.

6 Butter a 1½-quart soufflé dish, coat with Parmesan, and pour in. Sprinkle with Parmesan.

7 Place in oven and reduce temperature to 375°F. Bake for 35 to 40 minutes. Serve at once.

"...great for picnics or a quick lunch."

Vegetable Roll Niçoise

1 fresh, crusty French roll
1 tablespoon olive oil
1 large garlic clove, minced
  Anchovy paste *or* fillets
3 slices tomato
  Herb salt
  Fresh basil *or* mint leaves
  Sliced red *or* white radishes
  Slices of hothouse cucumber
1 teaspoon red wine vinegar
  Green leaf lettuce *or* other
  crisp greens
3 slices red onion

1 Slice roll in half and spread olive oil on cut sides. Spread garlic on bottom half and anchovy on top half.

2 Place tomato slices on bottom half. Sprinkle lightly with herb salt and top with basil or mint leaves.

3 Add radishes, then cucumbers. Sprinkle with vinegar and a little herb salt.

4 Top with green leaf lettuce, then onions.

5 Replace top half of roll.

6 Wrap tightly in plastic wrap and weight with a brick or a baking pan filled with heavy cans.

7 Refrigerate for at least 1 hour, removing weights after 30 minutes.

"One of my most popular side dishes."

Vegetable Gratin

6 to 8 servings

2 garlic cloves, minced
½ cup dark green olive oil
2 long baking potatoes, sliced very thinly
3 medium zucchini, sliced about ⅛ inch thick
9 Italian plum tomatoes, sliced ¼ inch thick
1 cup shredded Gruyère cheese
1 teaspoon fines herbes
   Salt and pepper to taste
12 leaves fresh basil (garnish)

1 Preheat oven to 425°F. Heat garlic gently in olive oil for about 5 minutes. (This may be done in advance.)

2 In a shallow 9 × 12-inch oval baking dish, arrange vegetables in alternating layers as follows: Layer half the potatoes, zucchini, tomatoes and cheese and sprinkle with fines herbes and salt and pepper. Repeat. Sprinkle with garlic oil and bake for about 45 minutes.

3 Meanwhile, stack and roll the basil leaves, then slice as thinly as possible into shreds.

4 When vegetables are tender, remove from oven and sprinkle with shredded basil. Serve hot or at room temperature.

" . . . a work of art, easily prepared and perfect for an elegant lunch."

Country-style Green Beans

1 **pound fresh green beans, trimmed**
6 **tablespoons olive** *or* **walnut oil**
2 **tablespoons red wine** *or* **raspberry vinegar, or to taste**
1 **teaspoon Dijon-style mustard**
1 **garlic clove, minced**
¼ **teaspoon superfine sugar**
½ **teaspoon salt**
  Pepper to taste
  Watercress *or* **finely sliced romaine lettuce**
½ **cup black olives (2.2-ounce can), sliced (garnish)**
⅓ **cup walnut halves, cut into halves or quarters, lightly toasted (toast 6 to 8 minutes at 350°F)**
  Pimiento *or* **red bell pepper, cut into narrow strips (garnish)**

1 Blanch beans, uncovered, in 4 quarts boiling salted water for 4 minutes. Test quickly for tenderness.

2 Using a colander, drain immediately and rinse under cold running water to stop cooking.

3 As soon as beans are cool, dry in a towel.

4 Make a dressing of oil, vinegar, mustard, garlic, sugar and salt and pepper. Adjust seasoning to taste.

5 Line either a shallow bowl or small dinner plates with watercress or romaine. Place beans on it, parallel fashion, and sprinkle with some of the dressing and with olives and walnuts. Garnish with pimiento or pepper strips.

"Curry has long been used in French kitchens."

Spiced Vegetables

6 servings

3 tablespoons butter
1 large onion, coarsely chopped
1 cup sliced celery (bias cut)
2 medium carrots, diced
1 small red bell pepper, thinly sliced
1 small green bell pepper, thinly sliced
2 medium zucchini, diced
½ teaspoon curry powder
2 tomatoes, peeled, seeded and diced
  Pinch of sugar
  Salt and pepper to taste
¼ teaspoon lemon juice
	1 Melt butter in large sauté pan. Add onion and cook 3 minutes.
	
	2 Add celery and carrots; cook over moderate heat 3 minutes.
	
	3 Add sliced peppers and zucchini and cook, tossing until vegetables are crisp-tender, about 3 minutes.
	
	4 Add curry powder and tomatoes and heat briefly.
	
	5 Adjust to taste with sugar, salt and pepper and lemon juice. Serve immediately.

" . . . a very attractive and substantial side dish."

Broccoli-stuffed Tomatoes

8 servings

8 **firm medium tomatoes**
  Salt and pepper to taste
1¼ **pounds (approximately)**
  broccoli, trimmed and cut
  into florets (reserve 8
  florets)
½ **cup sour cream**
⅓ **cup grated Parmesan cheese**
¼ **teaspoon (scant) nutmeg**
  Melted butter (for florets)

1 Top tomatoes and carefully scoop out insides, leaving ¼-inch shell.

2 Lightly salt and pepper the inside of each, then invert over double thickness of paper towels to drain.

3 Cook broccoli in batches in 4 quarts boiling salted water just until tender, 2 to 3 minutes. Remove using slotted spoon. Drain broccoli well and let cool 5 minutes.

4 Place in bowl of processor and puree. Measure 2½ cups puree. Add sour cream and Parmesan and process briefly. Season with salt and pepper and nutmeg. Preheat oven to 350°F.

5 Spoon broccoli into tomatoes, mounding carefully. Place in lightly oiled baking dish and heat for 10 minutes.

6 Sprinkle florets with a little butter and place one on top of each tomato a few minutes before serving.

*"The pine nuts and garlic add a
taste of Provence to this dish."*

Spinach with Pine Nuts

2 cloves garlic, minced

3 tablespoons dark green olive oil

1½ pounds fresh spinach, trimmed, washed and dried *or* 2 10-ounce packages frozen spinach, thawed and drained

½ cup pine nuts, lightly toasted (toast 6 to 8 minutes at 350°F)

Salt and pepper to taste

1 In large skillet, sauté garlic in olive oil until soft. Add spinach and cook until tender and fairly dry.

2 Add pine nuts and cook until moisture is barely absorbed.

3 Season with salt and pepper.

"I often serve this for dinner parties."

Stuffed Zucchini

2 small onions, cut into ¼-inch dice
2 medium carrots, cut into ¼-inch dice
2 celery stalks, cut into ¼-inch dice
2 tablespoons butter
1 small bay leaf
½ teaspoon (scant) dried tarragon
4 tablespoons chopped fresh parsley
¼ teaspoon salt
  White pepper to taste
¼ pound mushrooms, cut into ¼-inch dice
6 6-inch zucchini
2 tablespoons butter, melted
  Chopped fresh parsley (garnish)

1 Sauté onions, carrots and celery in butter for 10 minutes (do not brown) with bay leaf, tarragon, 2 tablespoons parsley and salt and pepper.

2 Add mushrooms and cook another 10 minutes. Remove from heat. Adjust seasoning to taste.

3 Drop zucchini into lightly salted boiling water and boil slowly until barely tender, about 5 minutes. Drain; cool under cold running water.

4 Preheat oven to 425°F. Trim stems and cut one slice from side of each zucchini. Hollow out centers, leaving a ³⁄₁₆-inch border of flesh; drain briefly. Brush with butter and season lightly with salt and pepper.

5 Add remaining parsley to mushroom mixture and reheat. Remove bay leaf. Fill zucchini boats.

6 Place zucchini boats in buttered ovenproof dish containing a scant ¼ inch of water. Bake for 10 minutes (no more) in upper third of oven. Sprinkle with parsley and serve.

"My mother's scalloped potatoes are legendary. This is my shortened version of her recipe."

Scalloped Potatoes Savoyard

6 servings

2½ pounds boiling potatoes, peeled and thinly sliced
4 tablespoons (½ stick) butter
Salt and white pepper to taste
1¼ cups shredded Gruyère *or* Swiss cheese, plus 3 tablespoons additional
1 cup beef stock
1 egg
½ cup sour cream
½ cup whipping cream
Parsley sprig (garnish)

1 Preheat oven to 425°F. Drop sliced potatoes into pan of cold water, bring to boil, and cook for 10 minutes.

2 Drain potatoes and dry on large towel.

3 Arrange overlapping layers of potatoes in casserole, dotting each layer with butter and sprinkling lightly with salt and pepper and cheese. Repeat layers, ending with cheese, reserving 3 tablespoons.

4 Bring beef stock almost to boil and gently pour over potatoes.

5 Bake for 45 minutes, covering loosely with foil if potatoes appear to be browning too quickly. When potatoes are tender, remove from oven.

6 For cream topping, beat egg into creams, add 3 tablespoons cheese and spread over casserole. Return to oven until golden, about 5 minutes. Garnish with parsley and serve.

"... a colorful, refreshing dessert."

Strawberries with Raspberry Sauce

6 servings

2 10-ounce boxes frozen
  raspberries, thawed
1 tablespoon kirsch *or*
  framboise (raspberry brandy)
2 baskets strawberries, hulled,
  dried and chilled
  Crème Fraîche (garnish) (see
  following recipe)
  Fresh mint sprigs (garnish)

1 Puree raspberries and sieve to remove seeds.

2 Add kirsch, stirring well.

3 Place berries in chilled individual dessert dishes.

4 Cover berries with puree and garnish each serving with a dollop of Crème Fraîche and sprigs of fresh mint.

Crème Fraîche
Makes 2 cups
3 tablespoons buttermilk
2 cups whipping cream

1 Place buttermilk in a small bowl. Whisk in a little whipping cream, blending thoroughly. Add remaining cream gradually, whisking until smooth.

2 Set bowl in a larger bowl of hot water to bring cream to room temperature. Remove. Let stand about 8 hours, partially covered.

3 When cream has thickened, stir it, then cover and refrigerate.

" . . . the ultimate chocolate dessert."

Grandmother's Chocolate Cake

10 to 12 servings
Make a day ahead.

10 ounces bittersweet chocolate
1 cup (½ pound) unsalted butter, (cut half into small pieces), room temperature
3 egg whites
5 egg yolks
½ cup superfine sugar
Powdered sugar (garnish)
Walnut halves (garnish)

1 Preheat oven to 350°F. Line an 8-inch round cake pan tightly with foil.

2 Melt chocolate with half the butter over hot water. Remove from heat for 2 to 3 minutes, then blend in remaining butter, cut into pieces.

3 Add egg whites and yolks, one at a time, blending well after each addition. Stir in sugar and turn into pan, smoothing top.

4 Bake about 25 minutes (cake will be very soft in center).

5 Cool to room temperature, then refrigerate overnight.

6 Sprinkle with powdered sugar, garnish with walnuts and serve cold.

" . . . a good dessert to follow a heavy meal."

Chilled Mixed Fruit Laced with Liqueur

8 servings

7 to 8 cups of at least 4 different fruits, such as papaya, pineapple, kiwi fruit, strawberries, cantaloupe and blueberries, *or* peaches, watermelon, grapes, cherries, apples and oranges, *or* pineapple, papaya, cherries, blueberries, strawberries and honeydew

5 tablespoons sifted powdered sugar

¼ cup orange liqueur

1 Cut fruit in a variety of shapes, such as dice, wedges, balls or discs.

2 Gently combine in mixing bowl.

3 Sprinkle with powdered sugar and again combine gently.

4 Chill thoroughly.

5 Just before serving, pour liqueur over fruit.

"These are really quick. I even serve them for breakfast."

Apple Tartlettes

½ **pound puff pastry**
4 **or 5 crisp tart apples**
2 **tablespoons sugar**
1 **tablespoon butter**
½ **cup apricot *or* apricot-
    pineapple preserves, sieved
    and warmed**

1 Preheat oven to 425°F. Roll out pastry as thin as possible and cut into six 6- or 7-inch circles, using saucer as guide. Place on baking sheet.

2 Peel and core apples and cut into thin crescents.

3 Arrange apples on pastry, pinwheel fashion, leaving almost no edge.

4 Sprinkle with sugar and dot with butter.

5 Bake for 20 minutes.

6 Glaze with apricot preserves. Serve hot.

Pears Belle Hélène

6 servings

3 firm ripe pears, peeled, halved and cored
4 tablespoons lemon juice
1¾ cups white wine
½ cup water
  Peel of 1 lemon, cut into strips
¾ cup sugar
1 teaspoon vanilla
1 pint vanilla ice cream

1 Place pears in 1 quart of cold water with 2 tablespoons lemon juice.

2 Combine wine, ½ cup water, remaining lemon juice, lemon peel and sugar in saucepan. Bring to boil, reduce heat and simmer for 5 minutes.

3 Remove pears from water and place in liquid, adding more wine and sugar if pears are not covered. Simmer gently until tender when pierced, about 25 minutes. Let cool in syrup 20 minutes, turning occasionally.

4 Place pears in shallow bowl. Boil liquid until reduced to almost syrupy consistency. Add vanilla. Pour over pears and chill well, basting occasionally. Remove lemon peel. Serve topped with ice cream and Chocolate Sauce.

Chocolate Sauce
Makes about 1 cup
1½ ounces unsweetened chocolate
  Dash of cream of tartar
  Dash of salt
¾ cup sugar
½ cup whipping cream
½ teaspoon vanilla
1½ teaspoons almond-flavored liqueur

1 Melt chocolate in top of double boiler over hot (not boiling) water. Add cream of tartar, salt and sugar, stirring to blend thoroughly.

2 Add cream and cook until thick, stirring occasionally, about 30 minutes. Remove from heat and add vanilla and liqueur. Serve hot.

*"My husband loves flan. He was the
inspiration for this recipe."*

Rum Flan

1 cup sugar
2 tablespoons water
1¾ cups milk
2 cups half and half
8 eggs
¼ teaspoon salt
¼ cup dark rum
¼ cup almonds, slivered and toasted (toast 10 minutes at 350°F) (garnish)

1 In small saucepan, melt ½ cup sugar in water over medium heat and continue cooking, swirling until liquid turns amber. Quickly pour into a warmed 1½-quart shallow baking dish and tilt to coat bottom and sides.

2 Preheat oven to 325°F. Heat milk and half and half together, stirring often with a wooden spoon, until tiny bubbles form. Remove from heat.

3 Beat eggs slightly. Add remaining sugar, salt and rum and gradually stir in hot milk.

4 Pour mixture into baking dish. Place baking dish in pan. Add hot water until halfway up side of baking dish and bake until knife inserted near center comes out clean, about 50 minutes.

5 Cool to room temperature and then chill in refrigerator several hours or overnight. Unmold and sprinkle with almonds.

"Beignets are very traditional and easy to make."

Apricot Beignets

12 apricots, fresh *or* canned, cut in half
2 tablespoons Cognac
3 tablespoons sugar
¾ cup all purpose flour
¼ teaspoon salt
1 egg yolk
⅓ cup beer, room temperature
2 tablespoons water
2 tablespoons butter, melted
1 tablespoon Cognac
1 egg white
 Peanut *or* vegetable oil (for deep frying)
 Powdered sugar (garnish)

1 Marinate apricots in Cognac and sugar for 30 minutes.

2 *For batter:* Sift flour and salt into mixing bowl; form a well and drop egg yolk, beer and water into it.

3 Stir just until flour is incorporated. Stir in butter and Cognac and set aside for 30 minutes.

4 Beat egg white until stiff but not dry and gently fold into batter.

5 Drain apricots and drop one-third into batter, turning to coat.

6 Remove from batter with slotted spoon and fry in 2 to 3 inches of hot oil until crisp and golden, about 3 minutes.

7 Remove with a slotted spoon, drain on paper towels and dust with powdered sugar. Repeat with remaining apricots, one-third at a time. Serve warm.

"Clafouti is the French equivalent of cobbler."

Blueberry Clafouti

⅓ cup blanched almonds, lightly toasted (toast 6 to 8 minutes at 350°F)

½ cup unbleached all purpose flour

⅓ cup sugar

⅛ teaspoon salt

3 eggs, whisked, room temperature

2 tablespoons unsalted butter, melted and cooled

½ cup Crème Fraîche (see recipe, page 105) plus additional for garnish, if desired

1 teaspoon vanilla

2 tablespoons amaretto

3 cups fresh *or* frozen blueberries

¼ cup sugar

1 cup whipping cream *or* extra Crème Fraîche (garnish)

2 tablespoons powdered sugar

2 tablespoons Cognac *or* 2 teaspoons vanilla

1 Preheat oven to 350°F. Freeze almonds, then chop by hand or in a processor or blender until medium fine. Leave in bowl.

2 Add flour, sugar and salt and process with on-off turns until mixed. With machine running, gradually add eggs, butter, Crème Fraîche, vanilla and amaretto, processing just until smooth.

3 Put berries in bottom of buttered 10-inch shallow baking dish and sprinkle with sugar. Pour batter on top.

4 Bake until center is firm to touch and a skewer inserted comes out clean, about 40 minutes. Cool until almost room temperature.

5 Serve with whipped cream or Crème Fraîche. If serving with whipped cream, whip cream with powdered sugar and Cognac until thick.

"This reminds me of my childhood when Grandmama was baking, and her house was filled with the aroma of apples cooked with cinnamon and nutmeg."

Normandy Apple Cake

16 servings

6 tablespoons Calvados or applejack
4 cups pippin apples, cored, peeled and chopped
2 eggs
2 cups sugar
1 cup vegetable oil
2 cups plus 2 tablespoons all purpose flour
1 teaspoon salt
2 teaspoons baking soda
2 teaspoons cinnamon
1 teaspoon nutmeg
¼ teaspoon ground cloves
1 cup raisins
1 cup coarsely chopped walnuts
1 cup whipping cream
2 tablespoons powdered sugar
2 tablespoons Cognac

1 Preheat oven to 350°F. Oil a 9 × 13-inch baking pan and dust with flour.

2 Pour Calvados over chopped apples; mix well and set aside, stirring occasionally.

3 Beat together eggs, sugar and oil.

4 In a separate bowl, sift flour, salt, soda and spices together several times.

5 Stir about half of flour mixture into egg mixture.

6 Combine apples with raisins and nuts and mix with remaining flour mixture. Stir into egg mixture.

7 Turn into pan. Bake for 1 hour.

8 Meanwhile, whip cream with powdered sugar and Cognac until thick. Serve cake warm or cold with whipped cream.

*"For a dinner party, I pipe the cream onto
the mousse for a more formal look."*

Mousse au Citron

1½ **envelopes gelatin**
½ **cup water**
1 **tablespoon grated lemon peel**
¾ **cup lemon juice**
6 **eggs**
1½ **cups sugar**
¼ **teaspoon salt**
2 **cups whipping cream**
1 **teaspoon vanilla**
2 **tablespoons powdered sugar**
Mint leaves, fresh berries, lemon slices *or* candied violets (garnish)

1 Soak gelatin in water 5 minutes, then place over hot water until thoroughly dissolved.

2 Combine with lemon peel and juice.

3 Place eggs, sugar and salt in large beater bowl and beat at high speed until mixture is very thick and light, about 10 minutes.

4 With beater at low speed, slowly add gelatin mixture.

5 Chill until mixture begins to jell.

6 Whip 1 cup cream until it forms soft mounds, then fold into the gelatin-egg mixture and chill about 15 minutes.

7 Pour into a chilled 2- or 2½-quart serving dish or 8 to 10 sherbet glasses and chill.

8 Whip remaining cream with vanilla and powdered sugar and swirl over mousse just before serving. Garnish with mint leaves, fresh berries, thin slices of lemon or candied violets.

Index

Credits

Photographer: Henry Bjoin
Food stylist: Birthe Foreman
Jacket and cover design:
   John Brogna
Book design: Paula Schlosser
Recipe tester: Lorraine Shapiro
Special thanks to: Rose Grant, Mary
   Nadler, and Sylvia Tidwell

The Knapp Press is a wholly owned subsidiary of KNAPP COMMUNICATIONS CORPORATION
Chairman and Chief Executive Officer: Cleon T. Knapp
President: H. Stephen Cranston
Senior Vice-Presidents: Rosalie Bruno (New Venture Development), Betsy Wood Knapp (Administrative Services/Electronics), Harry Myers (Magazine Group Publisher), William J. N. Porter (Corporate Product Sales), Paige Rense (Editorial), and L. James Wade, Jr. (Finance)

THE KNAPP PRESS

President: Alice Bandy; *Administrative Assistant:* Beth Bell; *Editor:* Norman Kolpas; *Managing Editor:* Pamela Mosher; *Associate Editors:* Colleen Dunn Bates, Jan Koot, Sarah Lifton, Diane Rossen Worthington; *Assistant Editor:* Nancy D. Roberts; *Editorial Assistant:* Teresa Roupe; *Art Director:* Paula Schlosser; *Designer:* Robin Murawski; *Marketing Designer:* Barbara Kosoff; *Book Production Manager:* Larry Cooke; *Book Production Coordinators:* Veronica Losorelli, Joan Valentine; *Director, Rosebud Books:* Robert Groag; *Creative Director, Rosebud Books:* Jeffrey Book; *Financial Manager:* Joseph Goodman; *Assistant Finance Manager:* Kerri Culbertson; *Financial Assistant:* Julie Mason; *Fulfillment Services Manager:* Virginia Parry; *Director of Public Relations:* Jan B. Fox; *Marketing Assistants:* Dolores Briqueleur, Randy Levin; *Promotions Managers:* Joanne Denison, Nina Gerwin; *Special Sales Manager:* Lynn Blocker; *Special Sales Coordinator:* Amy Hershman